ROBERT VICKREY
Artist at Work

ROBERT VICKREY
Artist at Work

By
Robert Vickrey

WATSON-GUPTILL PUBLICATIONS, NEW YORK

First published 1979 in the United States and Canada by Watson-Guptill Publications,
a division of Billboard Publications, Inc.,
1515 Broadway, New York, N.Y. 10036

Library of Congress Cataloging in Publication Data
Vickrey, Robert, 1926-
   Robert Vickrey, artist at work.
   Includes index.
   1. Vickrey, Robert, 1926-   2. Painters—
United States—Biography. I. Title.
ND237.V48A2 1979   759.13 [B]   79-13352
ISBN 0-8230-4580-3

Manufactured in Japan

First Printing, 1979

To my late father for not trying to talk me out of it;
to my children for being such good models;
and to my wife, Marjorie, for just being herself.

I would like to acknowledge and thank the following people: Scott Schutz, Hirschl and Adler Galleries, New York; Mary Gruskin, Midtown Galleries, New York; John Schram, for photographing some of my work; Ralph Gerstlé, for the movie photograph, and Kurt Vonnegut for his felicitous phrase.

CONTENTS

ALISA'S BUBBLES *tempera, 20" x 30" (51 x 76.2 cm). Courtesy Hirschl and Adler Galleries, New York.*

COBBLESTONES AND BALLOONS *tempera, 30" x 20" (76.2 x 61 cm). Courtesy Hirschl and Adler Galleries, New York.*

PORTRAIT OF THE ARTIST

I. PERSONAL HISTORY

Acousin of mine, the family historian, once gave me a large, embossed, leather-bound volume that traced my mother's family back through the ages. Page followed page of exquisitely hand-lettered lineage until I reached the final entry, which read (and I'm not making this up), ". . . descended from Duncan, murdered by MacBeth in 1040 A.D." I lost it shortly afterward. While perusing this dubious document, I failed to notice any "artistic" branches on the family tree, except that we seem to be vaguely descended from Charles McKim, of the famous McKim, Mead & White architectural firm. However, my ancestor was supposed to have been less than brilliant in his work. When his more talented partner, Stanford White, was shot in 1906 by Harry Thaw (a famous scandal), a contemporary wit was rumored to have quipped, "Thaw shot the wrong architect."

My paternal grandmother, however, copied morbid Victorian prints (*St. Cecelia Listening to the Fairies*, etc.), and my mother liked to paint watercolors of sleeping Mexicans with little *zzzzzzzs* escaping from under their sombreros. I have always felt that I had much in common with my grandmother. All her life people tried to tell her what to do, but she always went her own way. For instance, she packed a pistol in her apron pocket till the day she died. She used to shoot at people too, but luckily she was a poor shot. For many decades, she lived with my grandfather in a small, cluttered, maze-like house in Lawrence, Kansas, where she kept approximately two thousand dollars in one-dollar bills hidden in every book, vase, and teapot on the premises.

She was continually at war with "burglars," like some demented character from James Thurber. Her entire yard was carefully strewn with noisy tin cans and light bulbs. Most nights she slept next to her bedroom window in a chair. If any unfortunate trespasser wandered into her yard after dark, she would flick a switch beside the window flooding the yard with light. Then she would hold her pistol out the window and empty it into the yard, which was strung with piano wire at throat level. Needless to say, my grandmother was seldom bothered.

All the sash-weighted windows, on the inner ledges, supported delicately balanced milk bottles which came crashing down if any "burglar" managed to noiselessly navigate the yard and avoid decapitation. Still, my grandmother seemed to be troubled by a seemingly endless army of invaders. Eventually, she realized that there was only one "unprotected" entrance to the house: a small basement window just big enough for a large cat—or a midget. You see, there actually were some elderly midgets living next door. Years later, I visited my grandmother and saw the tiny window finally and effectively burglar-proofed by a neat row of small cream bottles.

THE BEGINNING OF MY ART CAREER

I began my own personal war with "burglars" when I was born in New York City in 1926. Shortly afterward, my parents were divorced, and I went with my mother to live near Reno, Nevada. With my stepfather we lived on a ranch realistically named "The Lazy Me." The brand on the cattle was the first thing I ever drew. Two years later my half-brother Caleb was born. Actually, his name was Caleb Van Heusen Whitbeck Jr., which I thought was a great name. Together, we had a wonderful time stoning rats in the barn, watching the pigs being slaughtered, and learning to ride a bike on a corduroy road. I also started to draw whenever possible. One work, I remember, was slightly obscene. I was scolded, "Why don't you draw something nice?"

Soon I was attending a one-room schoolhouse with a single teacher for all eight grades. We didn't learn much but we were allowed to draw and even *paint* most of the day.

When my mother died in 1936, I went to New York City to live with my father, who had resigned from the Navy to become an insurance broker. It is amazing that in all the following years he never tried to dissuade me from becoming an artist, even though he always found my work "a little puzzling." He eventually sent me to a fashionable boarding school near White Plains, New York. In those days it was considered unhealthy for growing boys to be indoors before five PM. Not being a Puritan, I soon found that I could crawl in the window of the art room and paint in decadent warmth.

During my "official" art classes the teacher showed justifiable disgust when I insisted on creating pictures of Mickey Mouse and Donald Duck on wood, their images outlined by nail holes. "Why don't you try something different?" she pleaded. Over the years I was to hear similar advice many times.

Soon I gave up my dreams of working for Walt Disney and decided that I wanted to become the Norman Rockwell of my generation. I started painting picturesque bums with chickens in hand being chased by ferocious hound-dogs, or picturesque barefoot boys being chased out of apple trees by ferocious straw-hatted farmers. I even painted picturesque Mexicans with ferocious zzzzzzzs escaping from under their sombreros. This lasted until I began visiting the Metropolitan and the Frick museums where I fell in love with Titian, Goya, El Greco, and especially Rembrandt. From then on, all thoughts of being an illustrator were banished from my mind. Sleeping Mexicans, picturesque bums, and ferocious farmers were gone forever. Later, when I finally saw Turner's original paintings, I began to worship him. I have been told that some of my half-finished pictures looked Turneresque.

Next, I was enrolled, with money from a generous aunt, at another fashionable boarding school with one considerable cultural advantage over the first: we did *not* have to eat everything on our plates. The year I arrived, art and soccer (my two favorite pastimes) were cancelled. Art was considered too frivolous in 1940, and soccer was luring too many players away from football, which was considered more important by the school. The abandoned art room was still there for unofficial, uncredited use. At least I didn't have to crawl in the window.

In 1942, however, the prospects improved when Victoria Huntley, a difficult person but a brilliant teacher, arrived at the school. Mrs. Huntley was a nationally known lithographer who seemed to look down upon this skill and yearned to be known as a painter. She began the laborious task of prying me away from my old bad habits, whereupon I promptly developed new bad habits. She used to sock me in the

This is one of the first things I ever drew: the cattle brand "The Lazy Me."

One of my first paintings, The Texture of Decay, *done at Yale around 1950.*

arm when I was too obtuse or unwilling to understand. My arm was sore for weeks at a time. I studied anatomy books and read everything I could find on "Art Theory"—whatever that was. I pored over reproductions of the Old Masters. And I plunged into the creation of a large, dreadful mural of a Civil War hospital camp with dying soldiers, rearing horses, and an entire platoon staggering in from one side. The school, I think, still hangs this item in a dark snack bar in the basement.

ART SCHOOL

Victoria Huntley continued to guide me, at least spiritually, for the next two years (my arm didn't hurt that way) while I was in the V-12 and NROTC programs (military training) at Wesleyan and Yale. At the latter, the Navy felt that art classes were "inconsistent with a serious approach to the war effort" (even though the war had been over for a year). And so I attended the Yale Art School life classes without credit.

There, I found some of the models rather interesting. Since I was a special student, I was occasionally left alone in the studio with a rather exhibitionistic model who often felt it was too much trouble to don a bathrobe during the "breaks." Another model refused to pose nude. One week she would pose in only her bra—and the next week in only her panties, but never nude. My favorites models were the non-professionals, since they were less "posey." One woman did not realize when she answered the ad that she was expected to pose "that way." After some hesitation, she decided to give it a try. Soon she started bringing in her friends, who were, of course "respectably married women." They told their unsuspecting husbands that they were doing cleaning and pocketed the extra dollar-and-a-half.

In my spare time at Yale I started another large painting, 6' x 18' (2 x 5.5 m), showing the top balcony of a movie theater. I worked in a then-abandoned dormitory in Nathan Hale's old room, although my painting protruded out the door, across the hall, and into the next room.

In 1947, I rolled it up, and after graduating from Yale University, I went to study at the Art Students League in New York under Reginald Marsh and *his* former teacher, Kenneth Hayes Miller. "Too flat, too flat," I heard every morning from Marsh. "Too round, too round," I heard every afternoon from Miller. I loved the League but I couldn't get any work done, since the students had to pack up all their gear every two or three hours and move, thus destroying any possibility of concentration. So, I went back to the Yale School of Fine Arts for two years. By then I was thoroughly committed to realism. From the teachers at Yale I began to hear the first of many refrains, "Why don't you try something abstract?" So it goes. Like my grandmother, I cocked my pistol and went my own way.

At Yale, however, I *did* learn about egg tempera! At first I didn't even want to take the course, since most students seemed to agree that it was a restrictive technique, allowing no room for improvisation and requiring laborious preparation, detailed drawings, tedious underpainting, etc. A typical egg tempera would be painted as follows:

LEARNING
EGG TEMPERA

1. A completely detailed drawing was done on toned paper. Cross-hatched india ink lines delineate the dark areas, while similar white-watercolor lines developed the highlights.

2. A tracing of this was made and transferred to a gesso panel. This could be done by "pouncing" or by using homemade or graphite carbon paper.

3. The original drawing was then recreated on the panel with black ink and cross-hatching.

4. Five values, from very light to very dark, of each color to be used in the painting were mixed in porcelain cups or the indentations in a porcelain palette.

5. The middle tone of each color was painted solidly over the entire area of the object to be depicted in that color, of course, obliterating all of the careful cross-hatching. Flesh, at this point, was flatly underpainted with a dull green.

6. All forms were developed by cross-hatching, the two dark tones for the receding areas and the two light tones for the advancing areas. Pure white could be used for the highlights, pure black for the darkest darks.

No wonder so few artists have used egg tempera in recent years!

After a short while, I began to see many different methods in the use of this medium. I asked many obnoxious questions about these possibilities and was usually answered with the reply, "It just isn't done that way." Finally, I moved back to my room where I could work out some of the ideas on my own.

FILMS

About this time I became interested in making films. I had always been a film buff, or as *Time* magazine would say, a "cinemaddict." This seemed the next logical step. At this point I had never even taken a still photograph, so I had to read a book about how to use a light meter, a tripod, etc. My first film was a modest effort: I chose to depict the end of the world. With my fellow students I shot multiple love scenes, a bombing, a fistfight, a murderous doppelganger, and, of course, suicide and resurrection. After some drastic editing, the finished title was *The Texture of Decay*. Ten years later I added a sound track made up of these sounds: a screwdriver held over rotating bicycle spokes, trumpeting elephants, air raid sirens, a celesta, etc. Over the next few years I made six more films with varying degrees of success.

AT YALE

After this initial foray into filmmaking, I turned once again to painting. I have always liked to work at night and was frustrated by Yale's policy of locking the students out at five PM ("for fear of orgies," we were told). I noticed, however, a small window with a broken lock in the men's room. So, every afternoon at five P.M. I would march conspicuously out the front door, wait ten minutes, then break into the school and continue my work for several more hours. Come to think of it, such a method of entrance into the contemporary art world seems to be the only one open to a realist. The authorities at Yale winked at such vagaries in the same way the Whitney Museum years later winked at our "dubious" activities and allowed us a small booth in their side show.

In 1950, Joseph Albers came to Yale as a visiting instructor and it soon became clear he was being groomed to take over the school. Albers, a famous hard-outline color-theorist, considerably influenced the Minimal and Op painting of years to come.

By the following fall, something of a political coup d'etat had taken place, and the majority of the excellent teaching staff of the school had been fired or forced to quit. I graduated before this happened, but not before the visiting Albers with his German accent suggested, "Vy don't you try something abstract?" So it goes.

I visited the premises the following year and noted that most of the student body was now painting in the "official" style. The halls were echoing with the accepted philosophy: "Mood iss a schvindle" (swindle), "Design and color iss all," "Execution iss unimportant," etc. At one point, I am told, Albers saw a neat but almost empty booth, called the students together, got down on his knees, crossed himself, and pontificated, "Zis iss Yale's mastervork." I was sorry to have missed that sort of thing. I suppose he would have flunked me, but I would not have minded. Besides, it would have been good practice for the thorny years to come.

Here I am pretending to be Cecil B. DeMille. I am shooting my epic production of Oedipus.

THE LABYRINTH *tempera, 24″ x 36″ (61 x 91.4 cm). Collection of The Whitney Museum of American Art, New York.*

I had been allowed to complete the five-year course in two years, and shortly after my second graduation from Yale I met and married my lovely wife, Marjorie. We set up housekeeping in Greenwich Village in a one-room, fourth-floor walkup. I painted in one corner (small pictures of course), and we cooked, ate, and slept in the rest of the room, heated occasionally by turning on the oven and leaving its door open, which upset the mouse feasting within. (We were sometimes startled when he'd arch across our bed in a perfect ten-foot parabola!)

I lugged small paintings and photographs of paintings around to several art galleries until I found one that would exhibit my work. I had a couple of shows there and managed to sell a few things. These sales and a small inheritance from my mother allowed us to move to a two-room Greenwich Village apartment, where I soon shared my studio-nursery with our first son, Scott. With more space available, I was no longer limited to small pieces. I submitted my first large painting, *The Labyrinth*, to a viewing at the Whitney Museum and was amazed that they not only accepted it for the next Annual but *bought* it. I was lucky enough to be in more than a dozen Whitney Annuals during the next few years, and they even made a postcard of *The Labyrinth*, which they displayed continuously in their lobby.

Meanwhile, I continued making short experimental movies; the early, simple, amateurish films gave way to the later, complicated, amateurish films. One evening an organization called Cinema 16 showed one of my films, and somewhat later the Paris Theater in New York showed one for five weeks. The audience did not like it, but one critic did. After winning some minor prizes, I felt that I was finally getting somewhere when a short film I directed and photographed, *Ellen in Windowland*, tied with a previous Academy Award winner (for second place) in the New York Golden Reel Festival. The film was favorably reviewed in the Sunday *New York Times*, which reproduced a still of the young heroine looking through a store window. No theater has ever been willing to show it.

During these years, however, "we happy few" realists who were acceptable to the Whitney were relegated to the "littlest room" in the museum, a sort of alcove off the main drag, almost an architectural afterthought. But we were thankful.

Later, the Whitney included me in their "New Generation" show of thirty-five Americans. At this point it became clear that the critics would never appreciate my brand of realism and they excoriated me for ignoring "the advances of abstraction." One critic even sent me cuttings of his reviews, in which he compared me to a "gorilla" and a "rotten apple." He carefully underlined his colorful references to me and signed the page with "Regards."

Actually, I have always liked much of the abstract painting of our time, especially the work of the Abstract Expressionists. In fact, when my paintings are half finished, viewers sometimes mistake them for abstractions. Then they praise me, of course, for seeing the light.

By now, I was associated with the Midtown Galleries, and after two more shows, Alan Gruskin, the director, informed me that my work was selling well enough for us to move to a four-room Greenwich Village apartment, where our first daughter, Nicole, was born. We soon had two more children, Carri and Sean, and moved to a six-room apartment.

WORKING FOR *TIME*

In 1957, an editor from *Time* magazine saw one of my figure paintings at the Whitney Annual and commissioned me to paint the first of more than seventy-five cover portraits. *Time* was very prosperous in those days. They sent me and sometimes my wife (first class, of course) all over the world on delightful expense accounts. I noticed in one of their telegrams I was officially "*Time*artist Vickrey." Soon I learned to take a compass with me on my assignments, since no hotel seemed to know which of its rooms had north light.

Working for *Time* was rather a bracing experience. Most people are surprised to hear that the magazine known for its prose editorializing never tried to influence the style or content of its covers. In fact, Otto Fuerbringer, known to the writers in those days as "The Iron Chancellor," was always very relaxed and friendly to the artists. He once told me to go ahead and be as unflattering as I wanted with Republican subjects, "because everyone knows we're a Republican magazine." Delineating the defects of the Democrats seemed to bring in the only criticism. Another editor who was extremely helpful to all the artists was James Keogh.

I gradually worked out a method of using egg tempera in thin washes on watercolor board which allowed me to paint a cover in one day—or in one night in some cases. Of course, some of these rush jobs were not my best work, and occasionally I even wanted to avoid signing them. If I tried to seek anonymity in this way, the magazine would print my name in clear block letters in the white margin at the bottom of the cover. I overcame this "favor" by signing my name in the lower left-hand corner where it was conveniently hidden by the address sticker on all of the subscription copies. Sneaking in the window again.

One of my favorite adventures in "*Time*land" (now I'm doing it) concerns my day in the life of John Kennedy. In the fall of 1960, *Time* commissioned me to paint the then campaigning senator. I was told that he could pose only on the plane trip between Chicago and Cleveland where he was speaking at an annual political rally. Since I would have only a few minutes of "posing" I decided to take photographs. As soon as I boarded his plane "The Caroline" I began to study Kennedy's facial planes, which were troublesome. Once we were aloft I sketched him for a few bumpy minutes, and then someone introduced me to him. He was friendly, but he seemed withdrawn and slightly upset. Finally, he said, "Aren't you rather young for this?" In days to come I thought of many clever replies, full of skillful but subtle references to his own relative youth, but at the time I only mumbled something like, "not really." After a pause he asked pointedly who else I had portrayed for *Time*. Not mentioning the sixteen covers I had painted over the years, I replied succinctly, "Well, Lyndon Johnson, your running mate." There was a long, cold silence and one of the aides said we'd better get on with the sitting.

Since most of the seats had desks in front of them, I had to lie on one of these to take closeups. Also, I found that my light meter was broken. Finally, though, with someone holding up a copy of the *New York Times* to reflect light into the difficult facial planes, I rolled around on the desk and managed to get a few pictures, in spite of the bumpy ride and the fact that I lost my light every time we went through a cloud.

Later, in Cleveland, when he started to speak I noticed that the tired, withdrawn look had disappeared from his face and he became the charismatic figure the world would soon know. He finished his speech to great applause and strode from the platform. I followed in a leisurely fashion and soon found that the entire motorcade had left without me. A flag-bedecked car rushed me to the airport where I hurried to the press plane, which was just about to take off. I realized that I had forgotten to eat that day and asked if there was any food aboard. No, they said, but I could have all the martinis I wanted. Safe with the knowledge that, after all, alcohol is a food, I winged my way home.

Back in my studio I began my portrait and soon found I was in trouble. Many artists have since found the same problems in representing the Kennedy physiognomy, especially the eyes, which would sometimes "lid" in a strange way that was almost impossible to depict. The facial planes would not stay in place. The cheeks seemed either too plump or too thin, changing from minute to minute. The mouth would smile, but the eyes would always look pained. As the deadline drew near, it became apparent the portrait was a failure. My wife said the man looked too sad. My son, Scott, felt that he seemed about to burst into laughter. The only part I liked was the hair.

The editors of *Time* quietly put the "thing" aside and for the cover used another portrait by a different artist. A few years later my portrait was returned to me, with no comment, in a plain brown wrapper.

In 1963, *Time* printed an article on rugged individualism in America. The editors had wanted to use Henry Luce (the founder of *Time*) himself on the cover but the great man modestly refused permission, and instead they chose Abraham Lincoln. They gave me every known photograph of Lincoln, and I eventually came up with a color portrait, part guesswork, part copy, and an entirely made-up right eye. After the cover appeared, at least three people inadvertently asked me if I had done it from a photograph. I thought this was quite humorous until I received a letter from a woman in West Virginia who told me that God was using the walls of her living room as a sort of private TV screen. The American Civil War was on that week, and I might, she said, be able to sketch Lincoln from life.

I also painted Lyndon Johnson when he was the Majority Leader of the Senate. He kept the *Time* photographer and me waiting in his office all day while he shook hands with a seemingly endless stream of constituents. We were finally admitted to his office just after sundown. It was quite dark, and we had to set up a photo flood to see him. After lecturing us for several minutes on the unfairness of all previously published portraits, he went into the next room where we could hear him shaving with an electric razor. He then announced we could have ten minutes of posing. Since we had been led to expect this sort of thing, we went into action. The photographer hopped about the room, taking as many pictures as possible while I attempted to sketch. When we got the photos back from the lab, we noticed that LBJ was coming out green. We guessed that the harsh lights and the after-shave lotion he must have used made him seem like something out of the *Wizard of Oz*. Still, when the cover appeared, he asked to have it.

After earlier turning down the chance to paint Vice-President Richard Nixon (no future there, I thought), I was commissioned to paint his wife, Pat. Mrs. Nixon was considered by the Washington press to be one of the most likable people in town, as indeed, I found her to be.

The architecture of the Nixon homestead in Georgetown reminded me of the house that Snap, Crackle, and Pop lived in. Checkers greeted me at the door; purposely, no servants seemed to be at hand. Soon Julie and Tricia arrived from school and pleaded with their mother to let them go to the movies. It was like "Ozzie and Harriet."

As the day wore on I noticed a trampoline outside the window where I was painting. Mrs. Nixon mentioned that when her husband came home in the evening, he sometime bounced about on this object with his children. She indicated that if I worked long enough I might be able to meet her husband and witness the festivities. Unfortunately, I was in a hurry and had to leave. To this day I am haunted by the fact that I missed the opportunity to see Richard Nixon tumbling about on a trampoline.

In 1967, Henry Luce died, and within a short while the atmosphere at *Time* changed. In 1968, I painted my last cover, the wedding portrait of Jacqueline Kennedy and Aristotle Onassis. I finished it in one night using old photographs as a guide. There was no picture of them together, and I suddenly realized at four A.M. that I didn't know who was taller. When I called New York no one answered, so I had to guess, and I guessed wrong. Jacqueline is taller, and when people ask me why I showed them otherwise I answer that they are standing on the stairs and Onassis is on the step behind her. Unfortunately, it was one of the fastest and worst covers I had ever done. One last time I tried to hide my signature in the lower left-hand corner where the address sticker would conceal my guilt. *Time*, however, abetted my anonymity by cropping the portrait and removing my name completely. As I said, this was my last cover to appear. Actually, I had painted one more, which did not appear: my "President" Humphrey portrait.

THE ART WORLD

Meanwhile, back in the dangerous thickets of the art world, we realists were still being hidden away at the Whitney. The museum, originally on Fourteenth Street, had moved to new quarters on Fifty-fourth Street, but had installed another, "littlest room" for us. Otherwise, we were more or less ignored.

Over the years, though, a few hardy souls had tried to let the world know what was going on behind the Iron Curtain of the "official" art world. For instance, in 1962, Hirschl and Adler Galleries in New York mounted a two-part show on American Realism in which I was included. But the critics, as usual, treated us like lepers.

UNDER THE SWINGS *tempera, 24″ x 36″ (61 x 91.4 cm). Private Collection.*

Suddenly, Abstract Expressionism pooped out, and New York was full of shadowy has-beens and fallen kings. What fad was next? The world waited. The answer came: The Figure. Did we realists get our hopes up? Perhaps for a few months. Then it became clear that the figures depicted must appear destroyed in some way—representing in short a cry of anguish over the Human Condition.

Pop Art followed. Abstract Expressionism wore its heart on its sleeve, but at least it had a heart. The new style was heartless. Ugly flash photos were copied with care. Billboards were presented with mock seriousness. Enlarged comic strips supposedly ripped the mask from the face of our shallow contemporary emotions. Dada was back, but instead of being a rebellion, it was the new official art.

While Pop raged about us, the Whitney included me for about the dozenth time in its Annual. John Canaday picked out my painting, *Under the Swings*, as one of the best in the show and reproduced it in the Sunday *New York Times*. Shortly after this I seemed to have been officially dropped by the Whitney Museum. But at least they still had my postcard on view in the lobby. With the mad persistence of my grandmother at war with burglars, I continued on my course as a realist, painting what I wanted and getting used to being an outsider in the art world. At least I had some company now—namely most of the Abstract Expressionists. New Realism for a while had a grip, an icy one, on the art world. Everything depicted seemed to be in a freezer. No warmth or life intruded. All figures seemed to be three days dead, full of formaldehyde, instead of blood, Torsos that appeared to be stuffed with sausage meat were praised for their "draftsmanship," knockwurst fingers were admired. Artist friends advised that I should put flat, strongly colored backgrounds behind my figures and chop them off at the knees. Then I would be in fashion. So it goes.

THE MOVE

At that time, the character of our neighborhood seemed to be changing. The walk from my studio to our apartment late at night was growing increasingly eerie. And one day I actually met a fastidious burglar face-to-face in our kitchen. He had stopped to clean up the mess he had made entering our window.

Shortly afterward, we packed up and moved to Connecticut. There, our two sons, Scott and Sean, and our two daughters, Nicole and Carri, grew into excellent models and began to show up in many of my pictures. Before this, my wife had posed for most of my figures and they had all looked like her.

WORKING AS AN ILLUSTRATOR

Over the years I have done a small amount of illustration, although I don't have the correct attitude for such work. Some magazines, such as *Redbook*, under the skillful art direction of Bill Cadge, allowed me to work in my own way and produce acceptable results. One year I even managed to win the Gold Medal from The Society of Illustrators.

An early adventure into this dark territory was a portrait of Frank Costello for *Esquire*. Their art director told me to paint him any way I wanted. "We love your work," he said. "Just make it as sensational as

possible." Taking him at this word, I portrayed the man and the wall behind him splattered with blood. *Esquire* dutifully paid me and commissioned someone else to paint out all my carefully rendered blood. A few years later *Esquire* called again, said they loved my work, and felt I was just the artist to paint a portrait of (are you ready?) James Bond's corpse, covered with blood.

At another time the *Reader's Digest* called and asked me to paint a cover for them. They offered a hundred dollars. I said no thank you. All right, then. A hundred twenty-five said the Art Director, feeling he had safely clinched the deal. I said I was awfully busy. "Don't worry," he said. "We'll have one of our staff artists design and draw it, all you have to do is to fill it in. By the way, we love your work."

Eventually, *New York* magazine called. After the usual protestations of love, a cheerful voice announced, "We have a job that would be perfect for your style." I sighed. "You see, we want a fine-art feel to it. It shows a Mafia murder, and all these blood-covered bodies are lying on the ground. . . ."

Perhaps I'll try something again with the sleeping Mexicans and the little "zzzzzzz's" escaping from under the sombreros.

MUSEUM CORRIDOR
acrylic, 24" x 36" (61 x 91.4 cm). Private Collection.

LATER YEARS

By now I was making a good living. In fact, one year I made as much as Mickey Mantle. My work had been acquired by The Metropolitan Museum, The Corcoran, The Brooklyn Museum, and more than thirty others. John Canaday of the *New York Times*, although he did not like some of what I was doing (and I agreed with him), called me "The world's most proficient craftsman in egg tempera painting." Shortly after this the *Times* stopped reviewing me. The Museum of Modern Art bought one of my works. A painting? No! A print of my film *The Texture of Decay*, which I had made while in school. The late Nelson Rockefeller tried to *give* them one of my paintings, and they refused to take it. In through the side window again.

Op (*Time* claims to have invented the term), Minimal, and Conceptual Art arrived. The "artist" had himself shot in the arm by a rifle, or he wrapped cliffs in plastic, or he caused little piles of red dust to jump into the air propelled by recorded heartbeats. By the seventies more doors were beginning to close. The newspapers stopped reviewing all but three or four hand-picked favorites each week. Most of the magazines that supported the illustrators folded or cut way back on reproductions. Publications that formerly reviewed realistic shows like the National Academy Annual and the American Watercolor Society Annual ceased to do so. A new law stopped the artist from taking a tax deduction from the donation of his work to charity or a museum. His heirs must pay taxes on unsold work at his death as if that work were cash in the bank. The art magazines now only reviewed a few select shows. A non-Pop realist, when looking at the art world today, is forced to feel a bit like Dorothy and her three friends when they saw the sign: HAUNTED FOREST. I'D TURN BACK IF I WERE YOU.

I've been lucky though, and like my grandmother I've lived my life as I wanted. There are still a few side windows left open. The University of Arizona Museum of Art and The Fine Arts Gallery of San Diego have given me large retrospective shows. Almost fifty museums have acquired my work, which is now handled by the Hirschl and Adler Galleries in New York. However, the Whitney has taken my postcard out of the lobby. I feel like a court-martialed officer stripped of his last epaulet.

For the first time, I'm beginning to get a steady stream of fan-mail. And I've just heard the first rumor of my death, "Vickrey, isn't he the guy who did all those bicycles? He's dead, isn't he?"

So it goes.

LIGHT AND REFLECTIONS *acrylic, 30″ x 39″ (76.2 x 99 cm). Courtesy Hirschl and Adler Galleries, New York.*

BEFORE THE PARADE *tempera, 26" x 40" (66 x 102 cm). Private Collection.*

My work has been described as "reality invested with images hauntingly suggestive, rather than visually explicit." Somehow I feel that my work *is* explicit, but explicit in the same way as a Kafka story, which explores in great deadpan detail something that does not physically exist. Another writer called me a "cinemaconologist" (i.e. one whose paintings look like scenes from films). This was meant to be an insult, but I took it as a great compliment. As one fascinated with moving images and shifting planes, I have made films influenced by my paintings, and paintings influenced by my films.

II. CONCEPTUAL
INFORMATION

Most of my ideas come with an element of surprise. I never had a dream that gave me an idea for a painting, but I have painted pictures that influenced my dreams. I have seen, in some form, most of the things I have painted, although I have changed or heightened them to make them more visual.

I have painted more nuns than anything else. I suppose I feel that the particular order I depict is the perfect fusion of a beautiful abstract shape and a spiritual anachronism, out of place in this Panglossian "best of all possible worlds." Most people do not see bicycles as elegant abstract forms (especially the shadows). I often show the bicycles in positions of danger. Old walls and pavement fascinate me because they are full of Turneresque tones and shapes, working against what man tries to make of them.

I have been told that my work has strong psychological overtones, and I guess it's true. Of course, I feel that daily life has strong psychological overtones, which I simply try to portray. I feel that I exaggerate about ten percent, which is enough to cause my work to be considered occasionally bizarre.

SHADOWS AND
IMAGES

If I paint a plant, I prefer to remove it from its natural habitat and place it behind a translucent curtain. There, if the sun shines on it, a distorted shadow is thrown on the curtain and seen through the curtain from the other side. When the plant (or person) rubs up against the curtain, dark spots (in the color of the object) are superimposed, shifted slightly, upon the shadow. Then I may show another plant on the near side of the curtain, creating an evasive, multi-faceted view of reality.

When I show a child drawing on the ground, he may be filling in his own shadow with white chalk, thus creating negative images of himself. Also, if he draws slowly, the shadow moves with the sun and creates a distorted image. I have been working for years on a painting of a young girl methodically filling in the shadows thrown by a single bicycle, which has been moved to different positions until the white negative silhouettes fill the entire panel. As an experiment, my daughter and I tried to trace the shadows of the bikes before the sun moved and changed them. We couldn't do it.

In another work the young artist comes upon a manhole while drawing his chalk maze. He simply incorporates it into the design (sometimes as a face) and proceeds on his way. Eventually, he will finish the elaborate maze—and find himself imprisoned within it.

TENNIS BALLS *tempera, 30" x 40" (76.2 x 102 cm). Private Collection.*

Right
TWO ROOMS *tempera, 16" x 12" (41 x 30.5 cm). Private Collection.*

A young girl on a city street may have just finished sketching a chalk flock of birds in frenzied flight. She has also just loosed a real bird from its cage to mingle (as seen from above) with the imaginary birds. The grooves in the concrete resemble the bars of the cage. One of the chalk birds seems to be in the cage. A pet kitten stands next to a chalk bird watching the real bird with great intensity.

Recently, I have been incorporating balloons into the mazes, since they can throw colored shadows. I also like stained-glass window patterns or complicated leaf shadows falling across the curved surfaces of nun's coifs or children's white hats. Though I can't figure out how to paint it, the most amazing shadow I've seen was of my head, while standing in the middle of the George Washington Bridge one night. Every hair, clearly silhouetted, was several blocks long.

WHERE I GET MY IDEAS

I often see things on the street, in theaters, on ferryboats, etc., which can't possibly be captured by sketching—I was never much good at it anyway. In such cases I either paint from memory or return with a camera, sometimes a movie camera. I'm not sure whether I'll end up with a film or a painting. I may take a hundred pictures and not use any one in particular. The mood (sorry, Mr. Albers), the textures, and the light are what I want to record. After I've done this research, I can start to change, to mold, to interpret. I seldom work from the model, except on portraits. I collect toys, balloons, and puppets, and watch the light falling on them from the windows until I find the exact time of day when I can see the effect I want.

I carry the simple compositions in my head. I allow the complicated ones (bicycles, shadows, reflections, etc.) to evolve slowly at their own pace as shown in the demonstrations. I keep photographs of manhole covers, battered walls, trees, etc., which I can use as elements when needed. Most of them have to be changed considerably.

SMALL TRAFFIC CIRCLE *tempera, 12″ x 16″ (30.5 x 41 cm). Private Collection.*

THE ATTIC ROOM *tempera, 24" x 36" (61 x 91.4 cm). Private Collection.*

THE ARCH AND THE SHADOW *tempera, 21' x 35" (53.3 x 89 cm). Private Collection.*

III. WORKING PROCEDURES

I seldom make doodles or rough sketches, and I never make a full-scale drawing, unless it is on the panel and executed in paint. Such a drawing, of course, is lost as the work proceeds. I seldom make studies in watercolor and never in pastel. I have no talent for the latter and gave it up thirty-five years ago.

Since I let each painting evolve at its own pace, I have to keep several going at the same time. If I change my mind halfway through, I scrape out the section I wish to change with a single-edge razor blade and sandpaper. At the beginning I usually paint the most important element in considerable detail. If this area seems to work, I go on. If not, I scrape off the whole thing and use the panel for something else. When only one part of the work seems successful, I save it, scrape the rest off, and redesign the whole thing. I once removed an entire painting, except for one eye, around which I then built a whole new picture.

Most of the time I know a painting will "work" from the very first day. Occasionally, I have ruined a painting that got off to a good start, but I have never been able to "save" one that got off to a bad start. I never know if an idea will work, so I just keep trying different ones out.

THE STUDIO

My first studio (the one with the parabolic mouse) was a small area next to the window in our one-room Greenwich Village apartment. Since I often worked at night, I had a reflector and a 150-watt blue daylight bulb attached to a stand behind me. During the day I would listen to the soothing misery of the radio soap operas; at night I would listen to classical music. This was a cheerful way to work, with my wife Marjorie embroidering clothes for the coming baby on my right, and the mouse occasionally watching from the windowsill on my left.

My next studio was a corner in my son Scott's nursery. Eventually, due to eccentric burglars and my three-year old son's attempts to improve my work, I had to rent a separate studio. There, from my delightful western-exposed window, I could look down onto Fourteenth Street and watch the illegal sidewalk vendors receive their tri-daily tickets from the friendly police.

A few years later we decided to move to the country for the children's sake. As I started to throw out all of the junk I had accumulated, my landlord asked if he could have some of the things. I said yes, with justified misgivings. Many years later he gave them to a museum and took a large tax deduction. The artist, under the present tax law, could take no deduction at all for such a gift.

Now we live on Cape Cod, where I have a large, cluttered studio with plenty of open shelves, discarded furniture, and a large, leaking skylight. At night, I use three 200-watt blue daylight bulbs and a 40-watt Vita-Lite fluorescent bulb, all "bouncing" off a white reflecting board.

When visitors (most are forbidden) first enter the studio, the floor may be covered with cast-off masking materials, drying paintings, pieces of acetate with discarded figures on them, balloons, paint-filled kleenex, wastebaskets full of water from the leaking skylight, etc. If the

hardy intruder is not allergic to dust, he may venture past the accumulated and discarded bureaus, tables, and shelves which are full of books, cans of films, photographs of paintings, a battered but working TV, a phonograph, and a tape recorder. The last three have wires running across the ceiling to the other side of the room where I sit at my easel, controlling the sound and gleefully turning off the commercials. Overhead is the skylight, valiantly but hopelessly preparing for the next rainstorm. On the wall to my left is the telephone with a cord that reaches fifteen feet, so that I can talk while walking around the room. Above the phone is the bank of assorted lights and reflectors, vainly attempting to simulate sunlight. Leaning against all walls, easels, and furniture are empty frames and half-finished framed paintings. The floor around the card table that holds my palette is covered with powdered pigment. This floor is also where my late, (often) rainbow-hued beagle

In the traditional "artist in his studio pose," I am pretending to paint. I am taking this picture myself with a hidden cable release and a rubber bulb under my foot—concentrating very hard because the mechanism doesn't work most of the time.

Here is my palette and table (cleaned up, of course). Notice the smorgasbord arrangement of paint. My rodent friend's favorite titanium white is in the lower lefthand corner.

used to sleep. I cleaned it up somewhat for these photographs, but perhaps I shouldn't have.

The clutter and mess of my studio surprises people who are accustomed to my "neat, precise" work. For this photograph, I have tidied it up a bit since its usual state would cause even the Collier Brothers (famous recluses who lived amidst clutter) to smile in their tidy graves. Most of the time everything is covered with a friendly layer of dust (I call it a patina).

Since I am a film addict, I often paint with the TV on. This way I can "take in" several films a day without leaving the easel. In between these subliminal cinematic adventures, I listen to the soap operas. I also have most of Shakespeare on tape. Many of his lesser works share certain characteristics with the soaps.

I can't find a sensible easel at any price, so I buy cheap easels, which I alter. I've always misspelled "easel." When I looked it up in the dictionary this time, I noticed that the word is derived from the Latin "asinus," or "ass for bearing burdens." Most easels are indeed asinine. The manufacturers of these objects take it for granted that all artists paint small pictures from a standing position. Consequently, the central supporting spine of the easel ends a good ten inches from the floor, while the ratchet that supports the crosspiece (until it breaks after a few months) ends several inches short of that. Using such an easel, even a standing artist could not paint the top section of a large painting. I have drilled holes in the spines of my junky easels every inch or so, into which I insert a Phillips head screwdriver to support the crosspiece. When I wish to paint the top section of a large painting, I turn the easel ninety degrees and *lean* the painting, which is resting on the floor, against it.

Over the years I have changed brands of brushes many times. Originally, I used Winsor & Newton watercolor brushes, but I found them too "fat" for my purposes. Then I used Art-Sign brushes—their points actually *improved* with age. Now, however, I use Strathmore watercolor brushes, mostly the No. 2. The point is amazing and really lasts. They are very expensive, though.

At an early stage I may use a bristle oil painting brush for stippling and a large housepainter's brush for splattering. I sometimes use small, flat plastic sponges shaped with scissors for rock textures, old walls, etc. A palette knife (not a painting knife) comes in handy for applying rough textures to simulate mortar or old posters. A painting knife is too flexible for tempera and applies the paint in too-thick gobs. Since the tempera layers must not become thick, I often scrape large areas down with the flat edge of a razor blade. The corners of the blade should be sandpapered until they are round, so they will not make grooves.

From time to time I cut out heavy paper masks, which are used to cover parts of the picture that I don't want to be affected by the sponging, splattering, etc.

Traditionally, the tempera palette has been a white, flat, nonporous surface with many small indentations, or cups, to hold many

EASEL, BRUSHES, PALETTE

carefully graded selections of local color. Since I don't work with local color and prefer overall tones and washes, I use a large AquaBee disposable paper palette (No. 6050). I don't use the disposable paper palette made for acrylic because the egg tempera paint will "crawl" all over the slippery surface.

PIGMENT

It is difficult to find pure powdered pigment. Grumbacher used to grind it in water for egg tempera painters, but this became unprofitable for them, and they stopped. Now I buy excellent (and inexpensive) powdered pigment from Fezandie & Sperrle, Inc., 103 Lafayette St., New York, New York. Of course, ordering it from them is an experience. It seems that the pigment goes up in price every few weeks, and the artist must order it by mail or phone several weeks in advance. The friendly correspondent from the company relays the latest prices to the artist, who promptly sends his check. A few weeks later the artist receives a friendly letter from the company telling him that the prices have gone up while he was waiting and they are requesting another small check to cover the difference. The artist in a frenzy sends a second check, air-mail special-delivery, and with a little luck receives his pigment several weeks later with a friendly note advising him that he just made it under the wire before the new coming price rise.

For years I simply poured pigment into small jars, added water, and shook it vigorously until it was a smooth paste. Now, in order to ensure an even smoother paste, I have it ground in water by my framer.

With a palette knife, I transfer dabs of this smooth paste from the jars to the paper palette. I arrange the colors in a smorgasbord-like semicircle from which they can be pulled into the middle to create new tones. At this point, I place a drop of water on each dab of color to keep them from drying out.

EGG TEMPERA TECHNIQUE

The paint will not, however, stick onto the panel unless the binder is added. That's where the egg comes in.

1. First, I crack the egg, and while the yolk is still in the half-shell, I drain off the white.

2. I place the yolk (still in its sac) on a paper towel and roll it around gently. The gobs of egg white will stick to the towel.

3. If the yolk sac breaks, no harm is done. If not, I puncture the sac with a pointed knife and let the contents drain into a small glass. I try to eliminate as much of the yolk sac as possible.

4. I add enough water so that, when stirred, the yolk-water emulsion is about the consistency of medium cream.

5. I place a piece of cheesecloth over the mouth of another small glass and strain the yellow liquid into it. I now have my egg tempera medium.

Some tempera painters use distilled water, which may be purchased at most drugstores. Recently I have been straining tap water through a

This is my wall with assorted drawings, marionettes, masks, telephone numbers, letters, and newspaper clippings tacked where I can see them. They make an interesting trompe l'oeil—I may paint them someday.

gadget called the "Water Thing," which can be ordered from Water Products, Inc., 450 W. Chapel St., Columbus, Ohio. This instrument has been used by our astronauts to recycle their precious bodily fluids—which is good enough for me!

Disposal of the unwanted egg white has always been a problem. How many meringues, angel food cakes, and daiquiris can one family consume? I've just read in the last few weeks that Andrew Wyeth has solved the problem by pouring this nutritious substance over his dog's food. I tried this on our dog Webster's dinner and received, over the uneaten meal, the longest and dirtiest look ever exchanged between beast and man.

EGG TEMPERA PALETTE

I use a very limited range of colors:

Cadmium Yellow Medium	*A very strong color. Great for warming up other colors. A pound may last me the rest of my life.*
Yellow Ochre	*A very weak color. Good for underpainting, washes, warming up skies. A lot must be used in order to have any effect.*
Cadmium Red Light	*Again a strong color. Necessary for flesh tones and, of course, red objects. A half-pound will last me the rest of my life.*
Cobalt Blue	*A strong color for glazing, but it has no body. A small amount of white, which kills its beauty, must be added to make it cover evenly.*
Cerulean Blue	*A recent addition to my palette. When mixed with cobalt blue it creates a rich blue which will still cover evenly. A lot is required, however.*
Ultramarine Blue	*A cold color. I use it only to darken the darkest areas of my other blues. It must be kept in powdered form until placed on palette, since it becomes rock-hard in a few hours when mixed with water.*
Viridian Green	*A fine but weak color. It will not cover evenly unless mixed with a lighter color which may kill its subtle tones. Good for glazing.*
Burnt Sienna	*I used to use Burnt Umber, but now I find this brown richer. It makes fine neutral tones when mixed with Viridian Green and Yellow Ochre and glazed over gray.*
Ivory Black	*A strong pigment. I only use it to darken other colors and to sign my name.*
Titanium White	*When thickly mixed with the egg yolk binder, it is excellent for covering. Fine for splattering and sponging.*

Some of these colors seem to be edible, by the way. I had a small mouse in my studio who became addicted to titanium white. He would crawl up the leg of my table while I was working, survey the smorgasbord of delicacies, and invariably start munching on a large helping of this favorite food. No matter how vigorously I shooed him away or sought to lure him to one side with cookies and Life Savers, the miniature titanium-white junkie would sit on the floor, glaring at me until I again became absorbed in the painting. Then he would scuttle up the table leg and head for his "fix." It was hard on his digestion, though. One night I left some Tums on the table by mistake. By the next morning he had eaten the whole package. It must have been pretty noisy behind the wallboards that night. His droppings eventually became pure white, like rice. It looked as if there had been a wedding in my studio.

The panels on which I paint are made from untempered Masonite covered with gesso. There are many formulas for making this ground, some with rabbitskin glue, some with gelatin. Some use precipitated chalk; some use whiting. All of these seem to be good, even the powdered gesso, premixed and sold in art stores. Do not buy it in liquid form, though. It will have been made with a plastic binder or some form of chemical retardant which can only harm your painting in the long run. I don't prepare my own gesso panels. I have my framer make them for me.

PANELS

I usually tone the sanded gesso panel with an overall tone, applied with a 2″ or 3″ (5.1–8 cm) housepainter's brush. The first tone has no white in it, but the second, thicker layer of paint usually has quite a bit of white in it. This second layer is not uniform in color and often gives the overall effect of a patchwork quilt. By the way, at the last minute I mix the powdered titanium white (not mixed with water) directly with the egg-medium to make the resulting paint as thick as possible.

If I am painting something with a lot of texture (rough pavement, tree trunks, etc.) I may splatter on some paint with a large brush. Or I may stipple it on with a very old, battered brush. Or I may apply it with a sponge or palette knife. All of these things will be clarified later during the demonstrations.

TECHNIQUES

If you don't like the effects you have obtained so far, wipe off the whole thing with a piece of wet cheesecloth. Sometimes when you are doing this, you will achieve new and unexpected tones and color combinations that you may want to keep.

Next, I may start to draw in the main elements of the picture with a brush, using mostly neutral tones. I may want to glaze at this point, so I pour a large amount of egg medium onto the palette and add a small amount of the desired color. When this is applied quickly with a large brush over the preceding textures and tones, truly beautiful effects can be achieved.

I use razor blades to scrape away top layers and expose some of what is underneath. At other times I use a drybrush dragged over the already-established textures to create rough, silvery tones. I may tap with the side of the brush to break up a too-smooth section of the picture. If I am not sure how something will look, I place a piece of very thin acetate over the painting. It will cling to the surface of the panel if it is rubbed against some cloth first. Then I try out my changes or additions. If they work, I remove the acetate and paint them onto the panel. If they don't work, I remove the acetate and throw it away.

Of course, as the painting proceeds, fewer and fewer of these methods may be used. In most cases, all of the final work will be done with small or medium-sized brushes, carefully controlled. Much of the beautiful, glowing effect of egg tempera comes through during these later refinements.

SOME DRAWBACKS OF EGG TEMPERA

A few drawbacks to egg tempera should be noted. First, it dries so fast that no slow blending, as in oil, can be accomplished. Blending effects can be achieved by glazing, wiping, scumbling, or stippling.

Also, for a short while the surface is edible. Some time ago, I was painting a portrait in a not-too-fastidious apartment. When I came back the next morning and looked at my handiwork, I saw that the cockroaches had eaten off one side of the sitter's face.

The layers in an egg tempera painting must be very thin. A thick gob of paint will crack and fall off. When putting on the paint with a sponge or palette knife, be sure not to apply it too thickly. As I said before, scrape it down with the flat edge of a razor blade. In most cases this will not change the look of the texture.

It is sometimes difficult to have fresh eggs handy at the scene of the painting. In most cases when I have to paint on location (that movie terminology keeps creeping in), I take a sealed jar of the egg yolk-and-water mixture with me. If I'm staying at a hotel, I can get the eggs from room service. When I was painting the Princess of Morocco for *Time*, I tried (in my bad high school French) to order eggs uncooked from room service. They sent me a steady stream of soft-boiled eggs until the kitchen closed for the afternoon siesta. And in Morocco, during siesta, *everything* closes—except, I suddenly realized, the bars. With the "royal limousine" (actually a five-year-old Chevy) waiting, I pleaded with the hotel bartender to sell me an egg at any price. He replied, through an interpreter, that he could sell me an egg only in a drink. My interpreter tried to explain that I wanted to paint a picture *with* the egg. The bartender understood that I wanted to paint a picture *of* the egg. Contributing to a still life appealed to his native culture. He smiled thinly and sold me the egg. The princess (like Queen Victoria) was not amused by my story or my lateness. When a photo of me painting the princess appeared in *Time*, my wife commented, "You finally got your picture in *Time* . . . and your shirttail was out!"

ACRYLIC

I have recently been experimenting with acrylic paint. I don't like it as much as egg tempera, but I find it effective for some things.

The brand of acrylic paint I use is Liquitex. I arrived at this choice after much soul-searching. It is also the only brand the local art store carries. I paint on four-ply rag paper prepared for me by my framer, since most illustration board, even though it's pure white on top, is mounted on some kind of cheap cardboard full of chemicals that may eventually damage the delicate rag paper. Whatman Board, handmade watercolor paper mounted on heavy cardboard, was the best of the commercial products. It has not been manufactured for years. If you can find some tucked away in the storeroom of some obscure store, buy it immediately. Don't bother with most of Greenwich Village and midtown Manhattan, though. As soon as it stopped being manufactured, I took a day off, went to every store in these areas, and bought every piece I could find—there weren't very many.

Liquitex comes in tubes, and I use it exactly like tube watercolor. The main difference is that it dries more slowly (especially if retarder is added to it), and the top layers do not "pick up" or wash off the underneath layers. Also, with addition of Gel Medium, beautiful glazing can be done, much like the egg tempera glaze. The main difference is that the egg tempera glaze sets in two or three seconds and is almost immediately unworkable, while the acrylic glaze takes a minute or so to set and a bit longer to dry completely. During the first few hours, thin layers of acrylic can be washed off with cheesecloth soaked in water. After, alcohol and a lot of scrubbing are required to remove these layers.

Again, I prefer to use the AquaBee Palette 6050 rather than the one for acrylic. I lay out the colors just as I do for egg tempera. They are:

ACRYLIC PALETTE

Cadmium Red Light	*Same characteristics as egg tempera.*
Cadmium Yellow Medium	*Same characteristics as egg tempera.*
Yellow Oxide	*This seems to be the same as yellow ochre.*
Cerulean, Cobalt,	*Same as egg tempera but they cover better. And (sometimes) Ultramarine Blue*
Burnt Sienna	*Same as egg tempera but it covers better.*
Hooker's Green	*The closest thing to Viridian in this brand.*
Ivory Black	*More of the same.*
Titanium White	*Same characteristics as egg tempera. Unpalatable to mice, however.*

I use acrylic when I wish to work in broader shapes and less detail. It is a good medium to use when building up thick impasto or indulging in more subtle blending, which egg tempera does not allow. Stippling, sponging, and splattering work beautifully with acrylic, but scraping with a razor blade does not work. The surface, when dry, is too tough.

I draw on the board almost entirely in paint, seldom in detail. Basically, I work from a middle tone in both directions, instead of from dark-to-light or vice versa.

Major changes in acrylic must be made by painting over the offending area, since it is almost impossible to remove the rubbery paint layer, even with alchohol, without harming the rag paper. As in egg tempera, I often give up on an acrylic when it does not come out the way I want it. Unlike egg tempera, however, I cannot scrape off the paint and use the surface for another painting. I put them aside, crop them, come back to them later—just as in egg tempera.

Most artists will say that a picture is finished when the conception is fulfilled, which is a long-winded way of saying that a picture is finished when the artist says it is. Like Degas, I keep fiddling with a picture until I force myself to deliver it to some place of destination outside the studio. Even then, if it falls into my hands again, I go back to work on it.

I keep about forty frames of different styles and sizes around the studio so that I can try several approaches to framing each work. This allows me to frame most of my pictures when they are partially finished. It also makes my studio more cluttered and maze-like, just like my grandmother's house.

KEY CORNER *tempera, 8″ x 10″ (20.3 x 25.4 cm). Private Collection.*

WINDOW PANE *tempera, 20″ x 25″ (51 x 63.5 cm). Private Collection.*

DEMONSTRATIONS

SKI HAT

Step 1. My son Sean is the skeptic of the family. He believes in questioning everything and applying his own solution. In this painting of Sean, I've tried to capture that look.

Using tempera and a two-inch house painter's brush, I briskly apply some random strokes of cobalt blue and titanium white, and scrub in some areas of yellow ochre. Next, using a palette knife, I apply more titanium white here and there to begin building up textures for a wall. At this point the picture has a "Turneresque," abstract look. I know approximately where the various elements will go; I keep the whole painting fluid.

Step 2. Here I define some of the elements of the wall, and with a blurred blue area I indicate where the head will go. So far, I've used my brush sparingly. Most of the textures are applied with a palette knife, although I keep the paint layers thin so that they will not crack. If an area becomes too thick, I scrape it down with the flat edge of a single-edge razor blade and still maintain the visual texture. I usually apply the light tones over the darker ones. To achieve some of the stone and mortar textures, I apply titanium white with a tiny piece of plastic sponge, cut with scissors to the desired size and shape. Some of the grooves and shadows are painted in with a small brush.

Step 3. To achieve the brickwork effect in the middle blue area, I apply off-white paint with the straight, sharp edge of the sponge to indicate the lines of mortar. I apply the light colored bricks with a palette knife, using its long, straight edge to delineate the brick's edge. Now, I place the entire panel on the floor and splatter it very lightly with various mixtures of blue and ochre. I define the outline of the head by clarifying the edges of the blue blur.

Step 4. At last Sean makes his appearance. He is still completely blue, and I intend to use this color as the underpainting for the flesh tones. I draw in the features with a dark, neutral tone (using a small brush now) and "pull out" the highlights on his face with white and a touch of cadium red. I'm beginning to get that skeptical look on his face now. I like the way his hair comes through the eyes and nose openings in the ski hat, giving him the look of a disheveled Sherpa. Now I concentrate on the head; I'll return to the background later.

Step 5. I settle on the final composition now and crop the panel to the desired dimensions. I warm up the light areas of the flesh tones with a light "flesh tone" glaze and darken the shadows with my favorite neutral tone, a mixture of viridian green, burnt sienna, and yellow ochre. There is too much blue in the picture, so I change the jacket to a brownish green. The expression on the face is just about right.

Step 6. Now, I develop the head more. I glaze down all the shadows, letting some of the blue underpainting show through to create optical grays. I think the hat needs some sort of design to liven it up, so I put acetate over the head and draw a possible design on it with white paint. It *does* look better.

Step 7. Detail. I remove the acetate and paint the design on the hat. Then I can finish the strands of hair coming through its opening.

THE SKI HAT *tempera, 18" x 22" (46 x 56 cm). Courtesy Hirschl and Adler Galleries, New York.*

Step 8. Here is the finished painting. I glaze down parts of the wall, refine the splatter, palette knife, and sponge textures with a small watercolor brush. I also add more designs to Sean's hat and carefully letter his name onto the name-tape over his right eye.

Demonstration Two

FERRY BOAT REFLECTIONS

Step 1. Years ago, I used to take my children on the Staten Island Ferry. In the late-afternoon light, I became fascinated by the reflections of people through the double-paned windows. The double panes and curved glass broke up these reflections into curious near-abstract shapes, making the figures seem to loom mysteriously through the dark areas of the reflected images.

I decide to use acrylic, since its slower drying time is preferable for blending the difficult passages. Also, I want to load in the impasto in a way that would be disastrous in egg tempera (heavy impasto would crack immediately and start to fall off). With 1¼" (3.2 cm) brads, I nail a large piece of four-ply rag paper along the edges to a piece of plywood (tape will not hold the paper in place once it starts to warp). I decide to tackle one problem at a time. I start with a series of Cezanne-like strokes, creating an all-over broken texture of all the colors on my palette, laying in what I know will be reflections, based on several photographs. Now the whole piece of paper is blocked in, with parallel horizontal strokes predominating. I know where I want the figures in the foreground, but I don't feel confident to indicate them.

Step 2. After experimenting with many different figures on acetate, I finally find two that function fairly well. Next, I move them around until they seem to work with the other elements. The nun on acetate has begun to lose its static-electric charge and is held in place by drafting tape. Also, I add another window on the left.

Step 2. Detail. (Right) You can see the different colors in the horizontal brushstrokes as I begin to explore the broken images reflected in the window. The forms within the cabin of the ferry are only crudely indicated.

Step 3. I trace the outlines of the two figures from the acetate onto the picture and fill them in with paint. My daughter Nicole has posed for the rather grumpy looking nun whose features are drawn in with a small watercolor brush and a mixture of burnt sienna and viridian green. The frames of the two windows have been roughly indicated. The child's head works better on the other side of the pole.

Step 4. I clarify the frames of the windows and add a new dark pole, allowing the former pole to act as a reflection in the glass. I begin to add color to the figures and reflections, scrubbing and glazing them over the underpainting. Next, I load in heavy off-white impasto into the light areas. I refine the structure of the window frames and paint the small boy's head in more detail.

Step 5. Now I add the people *inside* the cabin of the ferry, half-glimpsed through the glass. This is tough. The forms within must sometimes complement, sometimes counterpoint the reflected images *and* the foreground figures—not to mention the windows on the other side of the boat.

Step 5. Detail. In this detail you can see how I begin to refine and organize the various facets of the reflections. I try to keep them believable. The double-paned glass really does break up the images this way. I also add the reflections of the foreground figures.

Step 6. The painting is cropped, and I arrive at the final dimensions. I render the dimly seen figures within using enough clarity to make them believable, yet limiting the detail so they will not clash with the more defined foreground figures. I begin to add the lighted bulbs that burn inside the cabin all day long, plus the outside light and part of a sign at the right.

FERRY BOAT REFLECTIONS *acrylic, 30" x 40" (76.2 x 102 cm). Courtesy Hirschl and Adler Galleries, New York.*

Step 7. Here is the finished painting. The paper now lies flat against the plywood. The circles of the lighted interior bulbs are blurred, and I add several smaller interior bulbs. Hopefully, all of the conflicting and complementing elements pull together.

Demonstration Three

WINGS

Step 1. For years I've studied the light that comes through the cheap glass windows of the room next to my studio. In late summer afternoons, the shadows of the tree leaves are distorted by the sun and broken up into semi-abstract patterns as they fall onto the floor and walls. I wanted to see how this light would fall on one of my nuns. My daughter Carri posed in an improvised headdress, and the result was so fascinating that I have done several variations on this theme.

I start by nailing (along the edges) a piece of hot-pressed Whatman Board to a sheet of plywood. This time I try a slightly different approach to the underpainting. With bristle brushes and Liquitex acrylic, I broadly cover the surface of the paper with broken, almost cubistic, strokes of all the colors on my palette. At this stage, I leave quite a bit of paper showing through the uneven patterns of arbitrary strokes and blocks of color.

Step 2. The picture is moving ahead fast. I hardly have time to photograph the next step before it begins to look very different. I scrub in the cerulean blue over the under-painting to suggest the patterns of late-afternoon light coming through a window and falling on a blue wall. Next, I load pure white into the slightly wet blue paint to suggest small whorls and point of light, an effect caused by the leaves of the trees outside and by the flaws in the windowglass. I quickly sketch in a rough monochromatic head of my daughter Carri in a nun's habit. At this point the broken-colored underpainting still predominates the features, but the head is "coming out of the haze" faster than I expected. Now I begin to work out the masses of light and shadow, similar to those I observe in the room next to my studio.

Step 3. At this stage I concentrate almost entirely on the refracted light falling on the wall and the nun's headdress. Circular strokes of the brush indicate the spangles of light, which assume a diamond-like brilliance at this time of day. I use old watercolor brushes with the points scissored off to a flat stubby edge since there's no point in using new, perfectly pointed brushes for this donkey work. The pyramidal shadow of the headdress makes its appearance at the right.

Step 4. Using a crude mask of tracing paper and drafting tape, I cover the figure of the nun. I place the painting flat on the floor and splatter a light patina of cerulean and cobalt blue liberally all over the wall area. I show the mask half-peeled off to indicate what I've been up to. The splattered texture doesn't show up too well in the reproduction, but it is very clear in the original.

Step 5. I start to glaze down and clarify the shadow areas of the face with my usual wash of a thin mixture of hooker's green, burnt sienna, and yellow ochre (called yellow oxide by the Liquitex Company). I paint the shoulders in very darkly, so that I'll have my darkest dark to adjust my other tones to. I knew I was going to introduce the motif of the trapped bird (with wings echoing the wings of the headdress), but I'm not sure where the bird (and its echo-like shadow) are to be placed, so I sketch these two elements onto separate pieces of transparent acetate. I move these around until I get what seems to be the best arrangement of the shapes. I also clarify the shadows and patterns on the wall, keeping in mind that they must be kept reasonably consistent with the patterns falling on the figure.

Step 6. By scribbling on tracing paper with a soft pencil, I make crude carbon paper. I place this under the pieces of acetate and trace the outlines of the bird and its shadow onto the painting. I then fill in the silhouette of the bird with a dark-brownish neutral color and the bird's shadow with a mixture of cobalt and cerulean blue, lightened with a touch of white. I glaze some transparent pink over the nun's face and generally clarify the features.

WINGS *acrylic, 20" x 30" (51 x 76.2 cm). Private Collection.*

Step 7. Here is the completed painting. I carefully mask off the figure once more and splatter a *very* light patina of cerulean blue over the whole background. Finally, I glaze down the darkest shadows on the wall until they are almost as dark as the arms of the nun's habit. The lighted areas of the nun's face are brought out with a light, opaque flesh tone composed of titanium white, cadmium red medium, cadmium yellow medium, and a touch of cerulean blue. I refine the features with a small, pointed watercolor brush. The areas where the sunlight hits the bird are painted opaquely and then lightly glazed down with a warm tone. I define the bird's shadow areas with the neutral tone of the original silhouette, with a few details added. The violently warped Whatman Board has now "settled down" and once again lies flat.

Demonstration Four

THE YELLOW DRESS

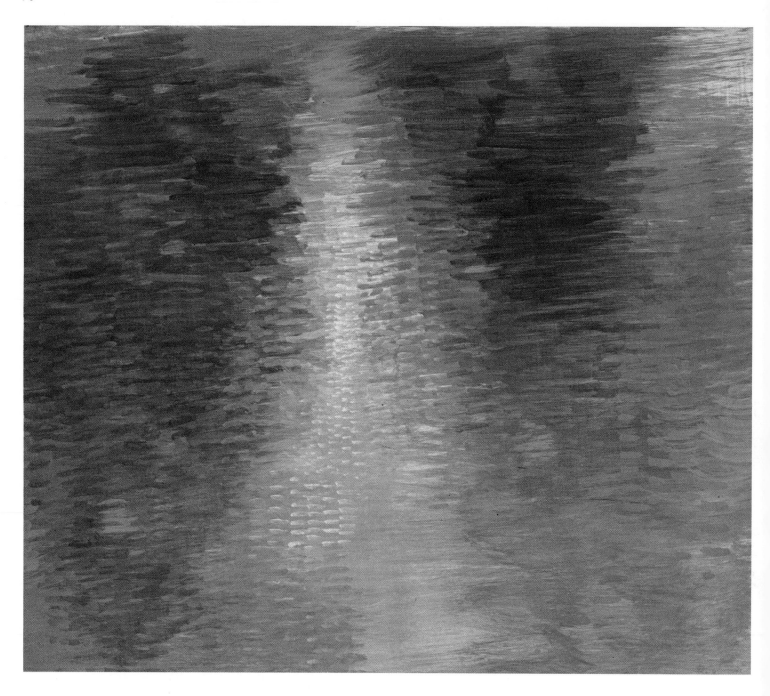

Step 1. For years I've painted my children's bikes lying in every possible position in strong sunlight. The complicated shadows and their interlocking shapes interest me even more than the images of the bikes themselves. One day, my children had carelessly left their bikes out in the rain. At first I was horrified, but then I noticed that the reflections in the wet pavement made delicate, blurred patterns as beautiful as the clear shadows. And so, after bawling out my puzzled kids, I proceeded, whenever it rained, to put the bikes outside in order to study them in detail. The wet pavement is the key factor in this painting, so I start to work on that first. I use tempera and tone the gesso panel slightly with a yellow ochre wash, and then with an old battered No. 5 watercolor brush I roughly indicate the masses with muted greens and browns. Then I load up the same brush with lighter colors (mixtures of white, cadmium yellow medium, cerulean blue, viridian green), and tap the side of the brush against the panel to create the slight impasto of the glare on the wet surface, where the light comes through the reflected trees.

Step 2. I paint in the outline of one bike, but right now I'm not sure where I want the others to go. I draw another bike on tracing paper and move it around until it seems to work in relationship to the first. Then I tape it into place. I want a more finished drawing than usual, and so I do not attempt to draw it on acetate with paint. By placing a piece of homemade carbon paper under the acetate drawing, I can transfer it to the panel with considerable detail.

Step 3. I remove the tracing paper and paint in the second bike. I start to refine the reflections and indicate where the crevices in the pavement will create puddles and distortions. Next, I glaze down the dark areas with thin washes of greens and browns. The spine of the painting, the central shaft of light, is now refined with fairly thick off-whites, tapped on with the side of the brush.

Then, I paint the third bike and figure on different pieces of acetate and move and move them around until they seem to work with the other elements. By this time the acetate has lost its static electric charge and is held onto the panel with drafting tape. On the wet pavement, I add a street line that forms something of a seesaw, with the light shaft and the central bike handle as a sort of fulcrum. Now I balance the bike on the left against the figure and bike on the right. At this point I feel that the back of a fourth bike (right) is required. (The acetate is fresh and thus stays on the panel with static electricity.)

Step 4. In simple flat tones I paint in the third bike, the figure, and the wheel of the fourth bike, all on the right side of the picture. The balance seems to be working fairly well (I crop the panel at the top).

Step 5. Now, I decide that the surface of the street is not clearly enough defined. To show the actual plane of the surface I add two expansion-joint grooves (in perspective) and a manhole to give a feeling of the flat concrete seen through the undulating shadows. I model the third bike, the figure, the plastic umbrella and its reflection in detail.

THE YELLOW DRESS *tempera, 20" x 24" (51 x 61 cm). Private Collection.*

Step 6. This is the finished painting. I add a few large leaves from the reflected trees— and another manhole (lightly indicated) to help the balance.

Demonstration Five

CRICKET'S PERCH

Step 1. A friend of mine has a dog named Cricket, a thin, nervous whippet, who likes to perch on a huge boulder near the house. I became fascinated by the sight of this tiny, fragile animal standing sentinel in this unusual setting. I wondered if I could balance such a light-weight shape against a pile of massive rocks, using his perch as a lever.

Using tempera, I begin by toning the whole gessoed panel with a light wash of yellow ochre, applied with a 2″ (5.1 cm) house-painter's brush. When this wash is dry, I load up the same brush with various mixtures of titanium white, cerulean blue, and yellow ochre and apply these mixtures with broad, arbitrary strokes over the whole panel. Next, I take an old No. 5 watercolor brush and roughly sketch in the dark shadow areas with a mixture of black and cobalt blue. Now I have my overall pattern, which I must begin to refine.

Step 2. I begin to glaze down the shadow areas with a wash of viridian green, burnt sienna, and yellow ochre. I cut up a plastic sponge into one-inch cubes, dip one of these into titanium white, thickly mixed, and dab in the highlights and basic rock textures. Things are starting to look up. When this dries, I place the panel on the floor, and using my old house-painter's brush again I splatter the whole thing with thin, almost transparent mixtures of all the colors on my palette.

Step 2. Detail. In this closeup you can see the various textures and forms I've just created.

Step 3. I decide to eliminate the sky, which is stunting and holding down the boulders. Instead, I plan to have the boulders rise in a sheer cliff. This will allow the figure of the dog (a silhouette painted on acetate and clinging to the surface by static electricity) to have a more clear-cut dramatic backdrop. I also begin to define the shapes and textures with a small No. 2 watercolor brush.

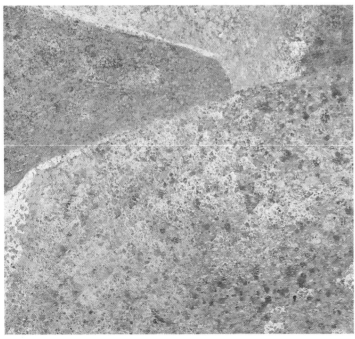

Step 4. The silhouette of the whippet is traced onto the panel and I paint it in with a dark neutral color. At this point I decide to utilize the whole panel and not to cut it down, as I often do. I still keep some of the rock shapes undefined, since I'm not sure of all the thrusts and balances of the masses, which seem to fall out of the picture on the left.

Step 4. Detail. You can see how I've altered the shapes of the rocks and refined the sponge-textures with small brushstrokes.

Step 5. Now things are moving swiftly. I change the shape of the rock at the far left so that it holds the masses back in the picture. The central cantilevered boulder is now fatter and less angled. I paint in more details. The shadow areas are glazed down with different neutral tones. And finally, I paint in grass, flowers, and vines to soften some of the lines.

Step 6. Now I start to paint the dog. The almost white highlights are quite broadly brushed in over the various shades of neutral gray. The original dark silhouette tone only shows between the legs. To make the dog's light, fragile shape stand out more clearly, I glaze down the cliff behind him with slightly darker tones.

CRICKET'S PERCH *tempera, 24" x 36" (61 x 91.4 cm). Private Collection.*

Step 7. Finished at last! I paint the dog in more detail and add his collar. Some of the things I've tried in this painting seem to work; others I'm not so sure of. For example, I could have balanced the rocks more exactly, but the equilibrium might be too monotonous. Overall, the painting seems complete.

Demonstration Six

ADMIRAL BENBOW

Step 1. After talking about it for 28 years, my wife Marjorie and I returned to England—the scene of our honeymoon. Once more I began my search for the perfect old wall to use as a background. On a rainy day we found ourselves in Cornwall wandering about the ruins of Tintagel Castle, searching for the grandeur of King Arthur, but finding only a few little walls two-or-three feet high and an occasional arch. As we drove through the nearby village, I spotted the most fantastic old building which turned out to be the original village post office, now, of course, surrounded by a modern garage, gifte shoppes, and trash bins. I took a few hurried shots of the structure. Later, back in my studio I began to think that the old "Admiral Benbow Inn" from *Treasure Island* must have looked something like that, and I decided to paint the wonderful building as it might have looked. The subtlety of the tones and the details of the stone walls seemed perfect for egg tempera.

I use tempera and first take a large gesso panel (which I know I'll cut down) and wash in a layer of yellow ochre over the whole surface with my battered old 2″ (5.1 cm) house-painter's brush. When this is dry, I use the same brush again to stroke, stipple, and scrub in varied mixtures of cobalt blue, titanium white, and yellow ochre, giving the impression of a cloudy sky.

Step 2. The sky in Step 1 is too blue and cheerful. I decide that I want it to be more dark and glowering, so I heavily load in a new tone with more black and yellow ochre in it, almost obliterating the original work. Now I get the effect I want. Then, I start to block in the ground and the building, with all the surrounding modern additions eliminated. I want the structure to be completely isolated.

Step 3. I crop the panel and develop the shape of the building. No details are put in yet, just a simple, almost cubistic shape. The small shed on the left and the wing on the right are silhouettes on acetate.

Step 4. I change the shape and position of the shed, but I'm still not sure of it, so I paint it again on acetate, together with the two hitching posts, and leave it in place a while. This delay causes the acetate to lose its static electric charge, and I must use drafting tape to keep it in place. I start to render the stone walls and slate shingles. The wing on the right is now painted on the panel, and the foreground is roughly indicated. I may show the sun (or moon) half-glimpsed through the cloud cover, so I try it out on acetate.

Step 4. Detail. You can see how I start to indicate the wall textures by painting in the light mortar between the dark stones. The sagging of the whole structure is an important element in the overall conception here.

Step 5. I paint the shed onto the panel. Next, with tracing paper and drafting tape, I mask off the sky and splatter the buildings and the foreground with a delicate patina of neutral tones (small amounts of burnt sienna, viridian green, cobalt blue, and yellow ochre mixed with large amounts of egg yolk medium)—just enough to darken it and give it a rough texture. In the few seconds before the spattered paint dries, I blot some areas with cheese cloth to make the texture more subtle. In the illustration I only half-removed the mask, so that you can see how I did it.

Step 6. Now I develop the cobblestones in the foreground, roughly block in the grass, render the shingles on the small shed, and add the trees on the left, the bench, and the distant sea. It doesn't show in the reproduction, but I also smooth out the rough spots in the sky, especially where it lightens at the horizon. I eliminate the sun-moon temporarily.

Step 7. I paint the sun-moon in permanently. I decide that the picture needs some indication of a human presence. It would be easy to add a small figure, but instead I paint an empty chair (with a view of the sea) on acetate and place it at the far end of the building. Also, I add trees on acetate to the horizon at the right. Those mysterious light lines are the wrinkles in the acetate catching the light.

Step 7. Detail. I start the final glazing down of the walls with a slightly darker neutral tone and a lot of egg yolk medium. On the side of the building you can see how I glaze from the top halfway down the wall. The bottom half is unglazed. For this step I use a very good No. 4 or No. 5 watercolor brush.

ADMIRAL BENBOW *tempera, 30" x 43" (78.1 x 109.2 cm). Courtesy Hirschl and Adler Galleries, New York.*

Step 8. Now I finish glazing down all the walls, paving stones, and cobblestones. I work on the grass texture with small brushstrokes, and I paint in the chair, the trees at the right, and two extra hitching posts for balance. I was adding a small flock of birds at the right and one large gull approaching the central chimney, when my son Sean came in and upon seeing the picture for the first time, said, "Change the gull to a crow, and you can send it in to 'The Twilight Zone.'"

ONE-MAN SHOW

ELEPHANT TREE *tempera, 20¼″ x 18⅛″ (52 x 71.4 cm). Courtesy Hirschl and Adler Galleries, New York.*

Years ago I spotted this tree in Connecticut. It fascinated me because eveything about it reminded me of an elephant. The trunk was like elephant's feet. The branches were like clusters of trunks and tails. The bark had that wonderful pachydermal skin texture. Over a period of years, I tried several different figures before I arrived at this final version.

THE FIRST DAY OF SPRING *tempera, 33½″ x 24″ (85.3 x 61 cm). Private Collection.*

A simple picture. I've painted a neighbor's boy returning to his favorite tree swing. He finds that the rope has broken and the tire has fallen into the melting snow where it protrudes as a dark, crescent-like image, which puzzles some viewers.

BUBBLES *tempera, 31″ x 43″ (79 x 109.2 cm). Courtesy Hirschl and Adler Galleries, New York.*

Backlighting is fascinating, especially as it comes through translucent bubbles and balloons. It forms halos when it is blocked by objects like the figures of the child and the cat in this picture. I love the way light falls on blonde hair, and I've painted this effect under all possible conditions.

Left
OLD MULBERRY *tempera, 20″ x 30⅛″ (51 x 77 cm). Private Collection.*

As you can see I love to paint old trees, rocks, and walls. They always seem to me like living people or animals. I can see several faces and figures in this gouty mulberry, whose battered surface could never be rendered successfully with the old traditional egg tempera technique. As you can see from this book, however, I have worked out methods of paint handling that allow me to depict these wonderful textures.

CECROPIA MOTH *tempera, 24″ x 36⅛″ (61 x 92 cm). Courtesy Hirschl and Adler Galleries, New York.*

Here is another painting that I worked on for years. I tried different patterns of light on the walls and different positions of the moths moving through them. I wanted the feeling of the nun held down at the bottom of the panel as if she were at the bottom of a well, while the moths floated above in seeming freedom. The large, formidable moth on the right is a simplified version of the Cecropia. The nun, occupied with her world below, is oblivious to the activity above her.

BIRD AT THE WINDOW *tempera, 24″ x 18″ (61 x 46 cm). Private Collection.*

I've painted many variations on the theme of a bird trapped indoors, a metaphor which has many meanings for me. Here I've only suggested the idea by showing the shadow on the wall behind my son Sean, looking older but no less skeptical.

SKIP ROPE *tempera, 18″ x 24″ (46 x 61 cm). Private Collection.*

I wanted this figure to appear to be escaping gravity, almost flying through the air against warm backlighting. But the kitten's curiosity firmly anchors both figures to the earth.

Left
TIGHTROPE WALKER *tempera, 26″ x 19″ (66 x 48.3 cm). Courtesy Hirschl and Adler Galleries, New York.*

My son is walking barefoot down the centerline of some huge street, balancing precariously as if on a high wire. The arrows go by like comets. The dotted line is like a vapor trail. The manhole cover might be a planet or star. The figure is silhouetted against the glow of light. When people tell me that the arrows are going the wrong way, I say the scene is in England.

THE LONG SHOT *tempera, 24" x 36" (61 x 91.4 cm). Courtesy Hirschl and Adler Galleries, New York.*

Here again I've used some of my favorite motifs: The long shadow, the patterned pavement, and the chalk drawing. Someone once (rather pompously) referred to this combination as: God's line, society's lines, and the artist's lines—farfetched but perhaps true. The kitten, however, is only interested in play.

LANDING CIRCLE *tempera, 24" x 36⅛" (61 x 92 cm). Courtesy Hirschl and Adler Galleries, New York.*

When I was young, balsa wood gliders were among my favorite toys. I painted several pictures of stacks of these small planes. In this version I'm playing the angles of the gliders against the octagonal pavement design, with the chalk circle as a confining element, from which, luckily, some of the gliders have escaped.

Above Left
GLORIA'S FLOWERS *tempera, 18" x 22¼" (46 x 57 cm). Private Collection.*

This is one of my favorite motifs: A child drawing on the ground with chalk. Here, instead of my usual dense, overlapping skein of lines and symbols, I've decided to try for the simplicity of the patterns in some of Gloria Vanderbilt's fabric designs—hence the title.

Left
BIRD CAGE *tempera, 16" x 12" (41 x 31 cm). Private Collection.*

The girl, in her own concrete cage (the grids of the expansion joints are like bars), releases her sheltered pet into a hostile environment. A "cute" kitten becomes a dangerous predator. The girl feels that she is freeing the bird, but which cage is safer?

DEIRDRE AND THE BALLOONS *tempera, 31″ x 43¼″ (79 x 110 cm). Private Collection.*

As I've mentioned before, I like to paint balloons because of their translucency (you can see their forms and yet see *through* them) and the fact that they throw colored shadows. At least, the cheap, thin-skinned ones do. Here, Deirdre is lost in a world of fragile, moving, colored shapes. The kitten, in its clumsiness, only destroys the shapes as it attempts to imitate her.

Right
BALLOON DANCE *tempera, 43¼″ x 30⅝″ (110 x 78 cm). Private Collection.*

Deirdre of *Deirdre and the Balloons* has now risen to her feet and is performing a semi-ballet with the colored spheres, as Chaplin did with the globe of the world in *The Great Dictator*. She weaves in and out of the sinous tree shadows, which advance toward her like unseen grasping hands. The balloons catch the sun and glow like lighted bulbs.

114

PORTRAIT OF SCOTT *tempera, 16″ x 20″ (41 x 51 cm). Collection of Remsen Scott Vickrey.*

This is a portrait of my oldest son Scott. He doesn't appear in many paintings since he has been away at school or work most of the time over the last fifteen years. He has a handsome, brooding quality which I have tried to capture here. He is now a film editor in New York.

WAITING *tempera, 20" x 30" (51 x 76.2 cm). Courtesy Midtown Galleries, New York.*

This is another picture in which I tried several figures and objects out before I arrived at the final combination. Some of these were on acetate, but I had to scrape out two large completed areas and repaint them because I was so dissatisfied. For some puzzling reason this summery scene ended up on a Christmas card.

MRS. MOORE *tempera, 20" x 30" (51 x 76.2 cm). Private Collection.*

I accept very few portrait commissions, and, frankly, very few people are brave enough to sit for me, since I am not good at flattery. Mrs. Moore, however, had such a strong, interesting face (which I enjoyed juxtaposing with the bold patterns of the sweater) that I felt I could paint a really strong character study. She is a painter herself and has reserved her opinion about the result.

Left
SHADOWS AND SEAN *tempera, 43" x 22" (109.2 x 56 cm). Private Collection.*

Here are more of my favorites. I wanted to emphasize the lengthening shadows, and so I chose a vertical shape for this. Sean is balancing on his toes and fingertips among the complicated shadow patterns, like a hang glider lost in the ecstacy of some inner world, which only he knows. Now he's twenty-two and has a truck.

MANIKIN *tempera, 32″ x 44⅛″ (81.3 x 112.3 cm). Courtesy Hirschl and Adler Galleries, New York.*

I have a small manikin that I use for studying cast shadows when they don't fall the way I want them to. It was carved in Italy and was ridiculously expensive, but it is so beautifully articulated that it can realistically imitate any human gesture. The above young lady was playing with it one day while resting between poses, and I decided to paint her just as she was. I didn't scrape out the previous painting this time, though. The plant shadows in the background are seen *through* the thin material of the curtain and played against the hanging ivy plant in front of it. We can see the bottle full of blue liquid pressing against the curtain, and we can also see some of its shadow.

CARNIVAL BOOTH *watercolor, 30" x 40" (76.2 x 102 cm). Courtesy Hirschl and Adler Galleries, New York.*

This is one of my latest acrylics. Since this kind of paint dries more slowly than egg tempera, I can blend the different tones and colors more smoothly to create the eerie glow of carnival lights (and their reflections) falling upon the shadowy, enigmatic figures crowding around the booth. I thought about this picture for more than ten years before I finally had enough confidence to start it. This is my third version.

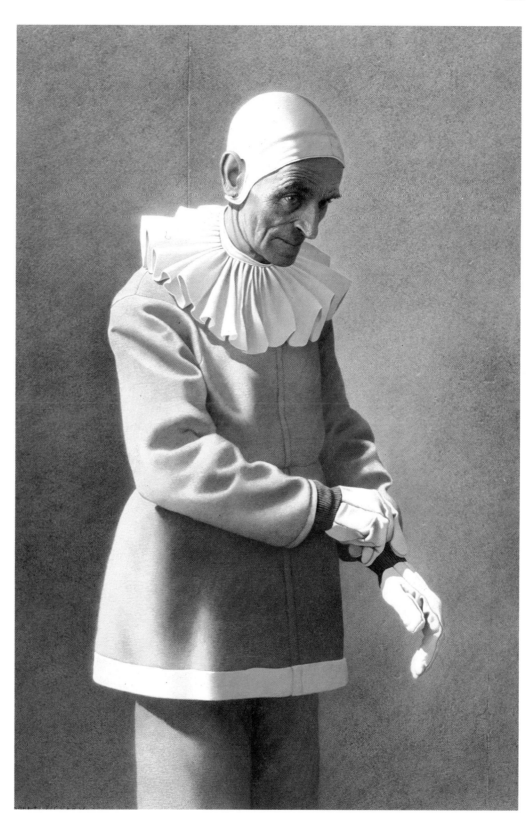

CLOWN DONNING GLOVES *tempera, 30" x 20" (76.2 x 51 cm). Courtesy Hirschl and Adler Galleries, New York.*

The pose in this painting came about by accident. The model was posing for a different picture. While he was taking a break, he started to pull on his gloves more tightly. I saw this, stopped him, and told him to stay just as he was. I scraped off the old panel and used it for something else.

SUMMER SHOWER *tempera, 18″ x 24″ (46 x 61 cm). Courtesy Midtown Galleries, New York.*

Another variation on the theme of bicycles and their reflections or shadows. The main problem here was the balancing of the small precise elements (figure, bike, and their reflections). You'll notice many manholes in my work.

AFTER THE STORM *acrylic, 12" x 16" (31 x 41 cm). Private Collection.*

This was about the third acrylic I painted. I should say *finished*, since I tried many times over the years and had to throw the unsuccessful results away. In this one I began to get command of the medium. I love the effect of a figure on wet pavement, seeming to float in space.

NUN IN THE RAIN *acrylic, 24″ x 36″ (61 x 91.4 cm). Private Collection.*

When a subject interests me, I do many versions of it. Rather than paint a landscape with trees, in most cases, I paint a reflection of that landscape. This way, I can break it up into new patterns caused by the uneven reflecting surface. The slight ripples in the thin layer of water covering the pavement are perfect for exploring this effect.

REFLECTIONS OF REFLECTIONS *watercolor and acrylic, 24″ x 36″ (61 x 91.4 cm). Private Collection.*

Here again I'm trying to investigate the shifting planes of reality, the clear, the half-hidden, and the deceptive. We see three nuns passing down a corridor that is lined with smooth stone slabs. We see the distorted, indistinct reflections on the floor. We also see the reflections of these figures (*and* their floor-reflections) reflected in the wall surfaces, plus a third reflected reflection in a plaque (far right) which we can't see in the actual corridor. The boundary lines between these areas are sometimes difficult to spot. I used acrylic here to depict the ambiguity of those passages that might seem too distinct in egg tempera.

STUDY OF NUN WITH POSTERS *oil, 72″ x 48″ (183 x 122 cm). Collection of Mrs. Robert Vickrey.*

This is the last oil I ever painted. It's really unfinished, but I felt that if I worked on it any longer, I would ruin whatever qualities it has. Now it hangs in my living room, where newcomers congratulate me on my advance into abstraction.

Left
MORNING LIGHT *tempera, 16″ x 12″ (41 x 31 cm). Private Collection.*

I'm fascinated by the way light falls on different surfaces such as rough, smooth, flat, curved, white, colored, etc. The subtle shape of the nun's headdress catches the straight, severe shutter patterns and bends them into graceful curves, all the time reflecting light into unexpected recesses in the shadow areas.

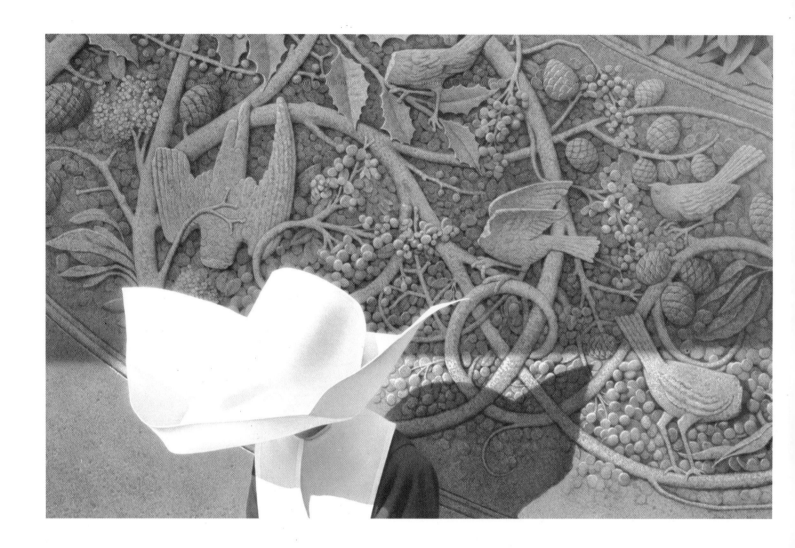

BIRD WALL *tempera, 20" x 30" (51 x 76.2 cm). Private Collection.*

For years I took my children to play in Central Park. There, on the stairs leading down to the boat pond, I used to pass beautiful bas relief walls. I was saddened to see them progressively smashed and sprayed with graffiti. Years later, I noticed all sorts of things going on in these decorations. Almost all of the birds' heads and some of the wings had been broken off, but still the headless figures dive-bombed into the lush thickets, gorging themselves (though headless) with stone fruits while grenade-like pine cones hung about them. The snake-like branches looked like jet trails but ended in twigs like barbed wire. The grapes reminded me of cluster bomb explosions. I decided to paint one of my pensive, faceless nuns turning away from the carnage. At the upper right a few actual green leaves intrude upon their carved likenesses. I've painted these walls many times, but I can't bring myself to show the graffiti.

THREE FROM ABOVE *tempera, 8" x 12" (20.3 x 31 cm). Private Collection.*

I've painted them from every other angle, so why not from directly above? The length-ening shadows delineate the figures. Here the nuns seem to be passing through chan-nels where the ubiquitous manholes lurk like mines, waiting for the unwary traveler.

THE VISITOR *tempera, 18″ x 22¼″ (46 x 57 cm). Courtesy Midtown Galleries, New York.*

I'm very fond of the distorted, refracted, sometimes elongated patterns thrown by the setting sun as it is filtered through the trees and the uneven glass windowpanes. I also love the way light falls on that particular white hat, which shows up in so many of my paintings.

Left
BOAT RIDE *acrylic, 39″ x 28″ (99.1 x 71.1 cm). Courtesy Hirschl and Adler Galleries, New York.*

This is a variation on the theme used in Demonstration Two. I wanted to try a vertical version of the ferry boat subject matter. Here I use acrylic on a Masonite panel, which was untempered and primed with titanium white. This surface allows me to work with considerably more detail than the paper used in the demonstration. The distorted figures reflected in the curved, double-paned window are endlessly intriguing, and I plan to use them again in future paintings.

DAYDREAMS *tempera, 20″ x 30″ (51 x 76.2). Private Collection.*

Here is Kim again, riding the back of a huge rock as if it were Moby Dick. In fact, the rock has several whale-like features; including that strange, upside down cetacean half-smile. The gulls give the feeling of that forward movement, which Kim feels in her mind.

CAROLINE'S BALLOONS *tempera, 14" x 18⅛" (36 x 46 cm). Courtesy Hirschl and Adler Galleries, New York.*

I've based three different paintings on the original drawing of my daughter in another of her favorite hats. She's the interior decorator of the family, and her walls are covered with all sorts of interesting objects. Actually, sunlight never enters her room, and I had to paint the balloons in a different place. I keep them hanging all over my garage in order to study the way it illuminates them.

CARRI IN THE RAIN *acrylic, 30" x 38" (76.2 x 97 cm). Courtesy Hirschl and Adler Galleries, New York.*

My daughter amidst reflections in a rainy street, bicycles, wet pavement, colored light patterns—all the things I like to paint. This even had a manhole in it, but I had to take it out because it was dominating the picture. I've used acrylic here. It seems better suited to the lighting effects with which I was experimenting.

VIEW OF THE SEA *tempera, 38¾″ x 35¼″ (73 x 90 cm). Private Collection.*

This is my son Sean—recognizable even with most of his head hidden. This is the first picture in which I explored the problems of depicting objects that are backlighted and also seen partially through a translucent curtain on which the objects cast shadows that are seen *through* the curtain. As Sean's hand touches the cloth, his shadow blends with the dark spots which are his visible fingertips. I tried to indicate the sound his left fist makes as he raps on the windowpane by showing the flustered birds outside. You can tell that I love to paint balloons and bottles of tinted liquid, since they cast such wonderful colored shadows.

CONNECTICUT GERMAN *tempera, 24" x 36" (61 x 91.4 cm). Private Collection.*

This is a house in Southport, Connecticut, but it looks so much like some of the houses in old German landscapes that I decided to paint it that way. As in some of my other pictures, I got the effect I wanted almost immediately—for half the panel. I scraped out two other detailed foregrounds before the layering of the ground plane seemed to work. I also had to eliminate several distracting elements such as a parking lot.

SNOWMAN *tempera, 24" x 34" (61 x 91.4 cm). Courtesy Hirschl and Adler Galleries, New York.*

This is another picture that I changed many times over the years. I wanted to see if I could balance the large mass of the foreground rock against the smaller elements in the background. After many tries, I arrived at this solution. The snowman of the title is almost unnoticeable in this reproduction.

KEY TO THE UNIVERSE *tempera, 24″ x 36″ (61 x 91.4 cm). Private Collection.*

The planet-sized hand unlocking the universe was an old insurance ad. For years, I pondered over the image before I knew how to use it. In this case, the universe has become a battered brick wall; the semi-divine hand of science has faded to a silhouette. The keyhole, the answer to all our problems, is only a tiny bricked-up side window. The nuns may have the answer; they are going in the opposite direction.

LEAF SHADOWS *tempera, 12" x 16" (30.5 x 41 cm). Private Collection.*

Shadows and more shadows—the beautiful, curved leaf shadows fall on the unyielding, rigid "grid" of the lines in a brick wall. The nun's headdress is intercepting the shadows, compressing and elongating them into new and wonderful shapes on the surface.

Right
WINGS IN PERSPECTIVE *tempera, 24" x 18" (61 x 46 cm). Private Collection.*

All lines lead down to the figure at the bottom. The nun's "wings" are spread for flight but seem to be held down by the invisible gravity. The perspective here is purposely inaccurate. When I first drew it in correctly, it did not give the effect I wanted.

COAST GUARD STATION *tempera, 24" x 36" (61 x 91.4 cm). Private Collection.*

The contrast of the abstract curves of the pipes and the straight lines of the building intrigued me. This old Cape Cod building still stands—or rather, floats. When I painted it, it seemed like a solid symbol of stability. However, as the years passed, the ocean crept up to its doorstep and began to undermine its foundation. Just before it sank, it was rescued, placed on a raft, and floated to Provincetown, where it floats on an uneasy berth.

INDEX

Edited by Donna Wilkinson
Designed by Jay Anning
Graphic Production by Hector Campbell
Set in 12/13 Palatino